DISCOVER "AMERICA THE BEAUTIFUL"

A Tribute to Our Nation

Cherry Lake Press

Published in the United States of America by Cherry Lake Publishing
Ann Arbor, Michigan
www.cherrylakepublishing.com

Reading Adviser: Beth Walker Gambro, MS, Ed., Reading Consultant, Yorkville, IL

Photo Credits: © Thye-Wee Gn/Shutterstock, cover, title page; © HalalStock/Dreamstime.com; Prints and Photographs Division/Library of Congress, 7; © bluejayphoto/iStock.com, 8; Currier & Ives/Prints and Photographs Division/Library of Congress, 9; © Ken Wolter/Shutterstock,10; © shironosov/iStock.com, 11; © joebelanger/iStock.com, 12; © Africa Studio/Shutterstock, 13; Remembering the Fallen by Chad Watkins/DVIDS/Public Domain, 14; © scyther5/iStock.com, 15; Unidentified Artist, Social Settlements: United States. Massachusetts. Boston. "Denison House": Denison House, Boston, Mass.: Settlement Houses (three), Harvard Art Museums/Fogg Museum, Transfer from the Carpenter Center for the Visual Arts, Social Museum Collection, Photo © President and Fellows of Harvard College, 3.2002.2979, 16; © Dan Thornberg/Shutterstock, 17; Hyland, C. C./Prints and Photographs Division/Library of Congress, 18; © Sanghwan Kim/iStock.com, 19; © SvetlanaSF/Shutterstock, 20

Cherry Lake Press is an imprint of Cherry Lake Publishing Group

Library of Congress Cataloging-in-Publication Data has been filed and is available at catalog.loc.gov.

Cherry Lake Publishing Group would like to acknowledge the work of the Partnership for 21st Century Learning, a Network of Battelle for Kids. Please visit Battelle for Kids online for more information.

Printed in the United States of America

Note from Publisher: Websites change regularly, and their future contents are outside of our control. Supervise children when conducting any recommended online searches for extended learning opportunities.

TABLE OF CONTENTS

INTRODUCTION

The wagon wheels creak as the horses pull them up the rocky path. Teachers from the Colorado Summer School are on an outing to Pikes Peak. It is July, 1893. The path is steep. The new railroad to the **summit** is broken, so wagons are their only option. Soon, they leave the wagons behind and switch to sure-footed mules.

One teacher is a visiting professor from Wellesley College in Massachusetts. She is hot and tired as they finally step up to the summit, but all that is swept away at the view. She is stunned. All the wonder of America seems laid out in front of her. She can see the fields of Kansas wheat. She can see the mountains rising around her.

“Oh, beautiful...” she thought on that historic day. Later, she would pen the first lines of a poem. She couldn’t know it then, but the words would be set to music and speak to the hearts of a nation.

Her name was Katharine Lee Bates, and the poem became “America the Beautiful.” It is a song that honors both the natural beauty of the country and its **enduring** promise of liberty and justice. It is a song still sung today with voices filled with pride from sea to shining sea.

"AMERICA THE BEAUTIFUL"

The song "America the Beautiful" was first published as a poem in 1895, two years after Katharine Lee Bates completed it on her trip to Colorado. It was soon set to music by Samuel Ward and played at events throughout the country.

O beautiful for spacious skies
For amber waves of grain,
For purple mountain majesties
Above the fruited plain!

★ **FAST FACTS** The lyrics "amber waves of grain" referred to the golden fields of wheat grown throughout the Great Plains. Today, U.S. farmers **produce** 1.97 billion bushels of wheat each year.

America! America!
God shed His grace on thee

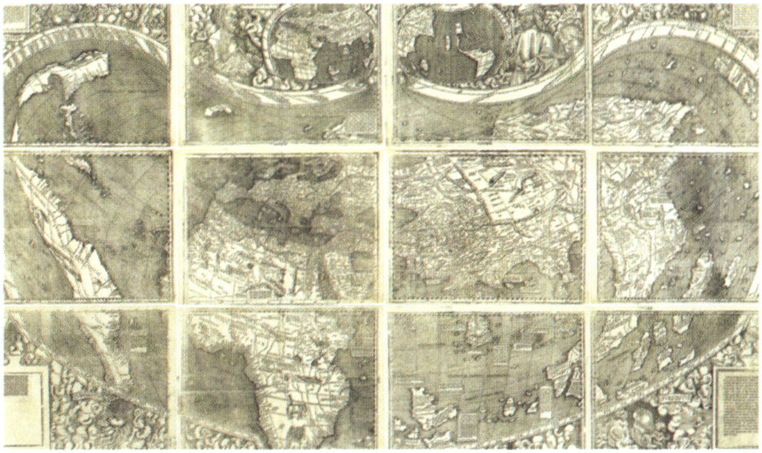

LOOK

What do you notice about the map?
Compare it with a modern world map.

★ **FAST FACTS** The Americas got their name from Italian explorer Amerigo Vespucci. Vespucci wrote letters about his travels across the Atlantic. The letters were published alongside a new world map. The publication labeled the newly added continents *America*.

And crown thy good with brotherhood
From sea to shining sea!

★ **FAST FACTS** The United States has coasts along the Atlantic Ocean, Pacific Ocean, Arctic Ocean, and the Caribbean Sea. Millions visit the coasts each year to experience their beauty.

O beautiful for pilgrim feet
Whose stern, impassioned stress

★ **FAST FACTS** The word *pilgrim* can mean a traveler to foreign lands. It most often means people who make a religious journey to visit a holy place. In U.S. history, it is also used to refer to the group of Puritans who left England and the Netherlands to create a colony in Massachusetts.

A thoroughfare for freedom beat Across the wilderness!

MAKE A GUESS

What do you think "thoroughfare" means? Make a guess. Then look up the word. Was your guess right?

★ **FAST FACTS** The National Wilderness Preservation System protects over 111 million acres of wilderness areas. These protected areas are set aside for all Americans and visitors to experience the natural beauty of this nation.

America! America!
God mend thine every flaw,

★ **FAST FACTS** Citizens have political power in democratic republics like the United States of America. They can organize for change. They can help make sure laws are **just**.

Confirm thy soul in self-control,
Thy liberty in law!

★ **FAST FACTS** The Constitution of the United States of America is the supreme law of the land. It sets the **framework** for the rest of the government and defines the freedoms for its citizens.

O beautiful for heroes proved
In liberating strife,

CREATE

Write a letter to a hero in your life telling them why they are a hero to you.

★ **FAST FACTS** The United States Armed Forces are the world's most powerful and most advanced military. Today, over 20 million Americans are veterans of the armed forces, having served American interests around the world.

Who more than self their country loved
And mercy more than life!

"[These men] summed up and perfected, by one supreme act, the highest virtues of men and citizens. For love of country they accepted death, and thus resolved all doubts, and made immortal their patriotism and their virtue."

– President James A. Garfield, 1868

America! America!
May God thy gold refine,

THINK

The poet is using gold as a **metaphor**. What do you think this verse is comparing to gold?

★ **FAST FACTS** Refining gold means to remove other materials from the gold ore after it is mined. Zinc, copper, and other minerals are some of those removed.

Till all success be nobleness,
And every gain divine!

★ **FAST FACTS** Katharine Lee Bates was committed to social reform. She opened a **settlement house** in Boston. She modeled it after Jane Addams' Hull House in Chicago.

O beautiful for patriot dream
That sees beyond the years

ASK QUESTIONS

Ask people in your life what "patriot dream" means to them. Were their answers all the same? Why do you think they were or weren't?

★ **FAST FACTS** The framers of the U.S. Constitution set up a process to **amend** the document. The Constitution could then change with the nation and the times.

Thine alabaster cities gleam
Undimmed by human tears!

★ **FAST FACTS** Alabaster is a soft, white mineral. On her way to Colorado, Katharine Lee Bates visited the 1893 Chicago World's Fair. Gardens, canals, and large exhibit halls were built to look like white marble. Chicago was nicknamed "The White City."

America! America!
God shed His grace on thee

★ **FAST FACTS** Katharine Lee Bates was a Congregationalist, a type of Protestant Christian. Her father was a minister. She was known to be deeply religious. This fueled her passion for social reform.

"Let us prove again that America can truly be a promised land, a land where people of every race, creed, and background can live together in freedom, harmony, and prosperity . . . from sea to shining sea."

– President Ronald Reagan, 1982

And crown thy good
with brotherhood
From sea to shining sea!

ALL ABOUT PIKES PEAK

Name origin: Brigadier General Zebulon Pike led an expedition for the United States and named it Highest Peak. It was later named Pikes Peak to honor him.

Indigenous name: *Tava-Kaavi*, "Sun Mountain" in the Ute language

Nickname: America's Mountain

Altitude: 14,115 feet (4,302.3 meters)

Location: Colorado

Range: Rocky Mountains

Visitors: Over 24 million each year

LEARN MORE

BOOKS

Bell, Samantha. *Exploring the National Parks*. Ann Arbor, MI: Cherry Lake Press, 2024.

Quinn, Jamie. *Discover "The Star-Spangled Banner": A Tribute to Our Nation*. Ann Arbor, MI: Cherry Lake Press, 2026.

WEBSITES

Search these online sources with an adult.

America the Beautiful | United States Navy Band via YouTube

Katharine Lee Bates facts for kids | Kiddle

GLOSSARY

amend (uh-MEND) to change or improve

enduring (in-DUR-ing) lasting a long time

framework (FRAYM-werk) structure of ideas; guiding principles

just (JUHST) morally good; fair

metaphor (MET-uh-for) a symbolic comparison

produce (pruh-DOOS) to grow or make for others to buy or use

settlement house (SET-uhl-muhnt HOWS) a place that provides community services for the poor in large cities

summit (SUM-it) the highest point of a mountain

INDEX